T0194715

SEARCHING

Discovering God's Hidden Treasures

Brooke Caldwell

WESTBOW
PRESS®
A DIVISION OF THOMAS NELSON
& ZONDERVAN

Scripture quotations marked (NLT) are taken from the Holy Bible, New Living Translation, copyright © 1996, 2004, 2007 by Tyndale House Foundation. Used by permission of Tyndale House Publishers, Inc., Carol Stream, Illinois 60188. All rights reserved.

This book is a work of non-fiction. Unless otherwise noted, the author and the publisher make no explicit guarantees as to the accuracy of the information contained in this book and in some cases, names of people and places have been altered to protect their privacy.

WestBow Press books may be ordered through booksellers or by contacting:

WestBow Press
A Division of Thomas Nelson & Zondervan
1663 Liberty Drive
Bloomington, IN 47403
www.westbowpress.com
1 (866) 928-1240

Because of the dynamic nature of the Internet, any web addresses or links contained in this book may have changed since publication and may no longer be valid. The views expressed in this work are solely those of the author and do not necessarily reflect the views of the publisher, and the publisher hereby disclaims any responsibility for them.

Any people depicted in stock imagery provided by Thinkstock are models, and such images are being used for illustrative purposes only.
Certain stock imagery © Thinkstock.

ISBN: 978-1-9736-1382-4 (sc)
ISBN: 978-1-9736-1383-1 (e)

Library of Congress Control Number: 2018900287

Print information available on the last page.

WestBow Press rev. date: 01/20/2018

Introduction

If you would have told me ten years ago that I would be writing a devotional book, I probably would have laughed in your face. You see, ten years ago, I was in a battle for my life: physically, emotionally, and most importantly, spiritually. The enemy had set his sights on me; he had intended to destroy me, my hopes, my dreams, and my future. So before I delve into the heart of this book, I want to give you a brief background of myself and the miracle you are literally holding in your hands.

Allow me to share part of my journey...

I was raised in a Christian home, married at a young age, and for as long as I can remember, was actively involved in my local church. Little did I know I was on a dead end road. I was doing the "right things," saying the "right things," living the "right way," but inside, I was a total mess and I was oblivious to the state of my soul.

God literally gave me a vision of myself walking down a dead end dirt road. When I finally realized that it was a dead end, I stopped, only to notice God right behind me. I asked Him, "Why are You following so close behind me?" He replied, "I was just waiting for you to stop trying to do things your way." I believe this was a vision of how I had been living my life, as well as many others walking with me on that same road.

I had to come to the end of myself. God allowed me to attempt to do life my way, but I floundered and failed. I turned around, only to realize God was there the whole time. He pointed me in the right direction, took my hand, and said, "Let Me go with you. Allow Me to take the lead."

It wasn't that I just woke up one day and decided to follow Jesus. Instead, I woke up one day to realize what a complete mess I was. I was broken; I was hurting, and I was out of options on how to fix myself. I tried to blame God, but that's like trying to fight someone who just wants to hold you. I tried to be mad at Him, but that's like screaming at someone who keeps telling you how much he loves you. I tried telling Him how He was ruining my life, yet He just kept pursuing me and telling me that His plans are better than my wildest dreams. He chased me down.

I have put off writing this book for many years. Fear of failure, fear of man's opinions, fear, fear, fear! Finally, I could not take it anymore. What I was feeling was not my fear at all; it was the Enemy's fear: afraid of the freedom it would bring me and also the freedom it will bring to others. It was his voice I was listening to, not my Father's. You will see as we take this journey together, one of the most critical mistakes we can ever make is listening to the wrong voice.

So as you turn the pages of this book, ask our Father God to make His voice drown out all the other voices screaming for your attention. His voice brings hope; His voice brings peace; His voice doesn't condemn; His voice is the voice of Love. How do I know this? I have experienced it firsthand. I know His voice, I have heard it with every fiber of my being, and I will never, ever be the same.

This book is what I see as treasures He has revealed to me along our journey together. It is stories of how He has shown Himself to me through Scripture I have read, through sermons I have heard, and through my own personal experiences. In the following pages are some of the most intimate conversations between a daughter and her Father.

I want to ask you to join me, to get a glimpse into the love that knows no limits and grab hold of the Hand that will always be reaching out for yours.

In Him lie hidden all the treasures of wisdom and knowledge. Colossians 2:3

"If you look for me wholeheartedly, you will find me. I will be
found by you," says the Lord. Jeremiah 29:13-14a

REST A WHILE

Then Jesus said, "Come to Me, all of you who are weary
and carry heavy burdens, and I will give you rest."
Matthew 11:28

I cannot think of a more fitting way to start a devotional than to partially unfold one of the most overlooked ideas birthed in the heart of the Father: rest. Rest is simply described as not moving, or as being in a resting position. It's a word often frowned upon because we generally link it to laziness, but rest is a part of God's plan for us.

How often have I made life more difficult than God intended it to be?

"Yes, Lord, I am weary. Yes, Lord, I am carrying heavy burdens. How can I obtain this rest that You speak of? What does it require of me, Father? Ten chapters of Bible reading? Hours in prayer? Perfect church attendance? Maybe a week long fast…or, oh no, a social media fast!"

Let's look one more time at Matthew 11:28. Right there, right at the beginning of the verse, straight from the mouth of Jesus Himself, one word: "Come." That's it; just come. All who are weary, all who are exhausted, all who are stressed out, come.

He is in control; I am not. He asked me to trust Him enough to rest. It is an attitude of the heart, a posture of my life that simply states, "I don't have to run around in a panic all the time; I have found my resting place, and it is in a relationship with my Father." We were not created to carry so much upon ourselves, always stressed to the max. We were made for the purpose of having a relationship with God. He wants to help; He wants to soothe and calm your heart; He wants to take your burdens; and He is just waiting on you to accept His invitation to come.

Father, show me what it looks like to rest in You. I give You everything that is weighing me down today.

What hidden treasure did God reveal to you today? _____

_____

What are some of your initial thoughts when you hear the word *rest*?

_____

_____

Do you feel *rest* is something you can achieve only at the end of the day or do you see *rest* as a lifestyle God is offering you to enjoy?

_____

_____

_____

What steps could you begin taking today to make *rest* part of your lifestyle?

_____

_____

_____

Your Prayer

_____

_____

THE JEALOUSY BUG

What I tell you now in the darkness, shout abroad when daybreak comes.
What I whisper in your ear, shout from the housetops for all to hear!
Matthew 10:27

Have you ever been jealous? What a silly question, because I am sure it is safe to say we have all been jealous at one time or another. But have you ever been jealous of another believer's walk with the Lord? Well, I have, and while I am laying all my cards on the table, I may as well get it out there in the open. I was actually jealous of how God was clearly working in my own husband's life. I know! It sounds awful, does it not? God was answering prayers-big prayers! In one week, God's hand was so evident in his life that I started sulking. I knew my husband was going to do as he always does: he would brag about God and tell everyone he possibly could how amazing his God is. That is his personality; he is very vocal about his faith. So as he was in the middle of bragging about God, the old jealousy bug got a hold of me.

"God," I asked, "why do You do all these amazing things, these awesome things that are very evident to so many people? Why do they happen to my husband and not to me? Why, Father? Is there something more special about him than me?" Now while I have never heard the audible voice of my Father, I instantly heard Him respond to my spirit, "Brooke, I shout my love to Steven, but I whisper my love to you." In that single moment, I felt God saying that yes, He saw me. Yes, He loves me and yes, He is answering my prayers every single day - but I should stop comparing His love for Steven with His love for me. While His love for us is the same, He speaks to us very differently based on our different personalities.

Jeremiah 31:3 says, "I have loved you, my people, with an everlasting love. With unfailing love I have drawn you to myself."

Is there anything more powerful, more substantial, or more amazing than the love of the Father? This is no ordinary love. God's love moves past those ugly, broken places in my own heart and life, and it compels me to look into the eyes of my Father. As I look into His eyes, I realize that it was His love that drew me to Himself, and it is His love that keeps me there.

We have no right to be jealous of another believer's walk. It is their own, personal walk, because our God is a personal God. Listen to Him speaking His love to you today, and let all those other voices just fade into the background.

Father, how are You expressing Your love for me today? Forgive
me for falling into the comparison trap. Help me to see You and to
hear You, as you affectionately pour out Your love for me.

What hidden treasures did God reveal to you today? _____

_____

Based on your own personality, how do you believe God can speak to you?

_____

_____

_____

Have you been guilty of comparing your spiritual journey with someone else's journey? Do you see the danger in this? Why or why not?

_____

_____

_____

Read Jeremiah 31:3 again and consider all the ways God's love has drawn you to Himself. Take a moment to reflect on that.

_____

_____

_____

Your Prayer

_____

_____

MINDCRAFT

Fix your thoughts on what is true, and honorable, and right, and pure, and lovely,
and admirable. Think about things that are excellent and worthy of praise.
Philippians 4:8

It seems like my mind is constantly working, thinking, planning, worrying, and, of course, daydreaming. Most of our battles are fought, won, and lost in our minds. Paul knew this, and when he wrote a letter to the Philippians, he gave them a guideline on what they should allow to consume their minds and thoughts. We can still use this same guideline for ourselves today:

Is what I'm thinking about true; is it honorable, and right? Is this a pure thought, a lovely, and admirable thought? If it is not, then it does not belong in our minds!

God wants us to control what goes on in our minds and what we spend time dwelling on. Picture your mind being a battlefield and imagine you are on the frontlines, standing guard, with sword drawn. You are the only one who can give access to those thoughts that bombard you throughout your day.

Psalm 104:35 says, "May all my thoughts be pleasing to him."

Wow, the psalmist said that he wanted *all* his thoughts to please God. After I read a verse like that, I'm thinking I have a long way to go!

In His wisdom, God allows us to choose our thoughts. He allows us to decide on what we give those precious moments to. God did not make us robots programmed to serve Him and to love Him. His desire is for us to set our thoughts on Him because we choose to. When our minds and thoughts are fixed on Him, we desire to please Him, and actions soon follow. We begin serving others, loving others from a genuine heart, a heart and life that is confident in who they are and whose they are.

Second Corinthians 10:5 says to take captive every thought and make each one obedient unto Christ. As believers in Christ, we need to focus more and more on what we are allowing to come into our minds. We have the power and authority to cast out those thoughts that are not pleasing to our Father.

Father, help me to be more aware of the thoughts that are contending for my attention. Today I choose to set my mind on You.

What hidden treasure did God reveal to you today? _____

_____

Did you connect with the idea of our minds being a battlefield? Explain

_____

_____

_____

Will Philippians 4:8 be a guideline that you could see yourself using as a reference to the thoughts being allowed into your mind?

_____

_____

Take a few moments to meditate on Psalm 104:35
"May all my thoughts be pleasing to him."

Your Prayer

_____

_____

STUDY TIME

For the word of God is alive and powerful. It is sharper than the
sharpest two-edged sword, cutting between soul and spirit, between
joint and marrow. It exposes our innermost thoughts and desires.
Hebrews 4:12

God's Word is vital to an intimate relationship with Jesus Christ. It is not just a devotional book or a history book; it is God's love letter to the human race. His Word is alive; His Word is for this present day just as much as it was for generations past and generations to come.

I have a few secrets that have helped me understand scripture better: One, before I even open the Bible, I try to remember to ask God to speak to me. Oh, how He loves to hear that request! "Father God, here I am. I am setting aside this time to listen to You, to open Your Word. Will you speak to me? Help me to hear Your voice and understand."

Second, I take a passage and then I personalize it. For instance, one of my favorite verses is Proverbs 3:5-6, which says,

"Trust in the LORD with all your heart; do not depend on your own understanding.
Seek his will in all you do, and he will show you which path to take."

Here is an example of how to personalize it: "Lord, with everything in me, with all that I am, I trust You. From my perspective, life isn't going how I planned. I am hurting and

I feel alone, but I know I cannot always trust my feelings. You are perfect, and You don't make mistakes. Show me how to seek You, show me how to trust You in the midst of all these other feelings. As I lean into You more and more, make my path clearer. Lead me and guide me today."

And last, God loves it when we read His Word back to Him. Using the same verses from Proverbs, we can pray with authority, "Lord, You said that if I trust You and if I would seek You, that You would show me which path to take." We are the sons and the daughters of the most high God. The King of all kings is our Father, and because we bear His Name, because we are heirs to a Heavenly Kingdom, we have the authority to bring that kingdom to earth. We will do it by using the powerful Word of God.

Father, forgive me for not honoring Your Word. I want to start hiding Your Word in my heart that I will not sin against You. I want to know You in a more intimate way. Will You please guide me and be my Teacher?

What hidden treasure did God reveal to you today? _____

_____

How do you view God's Word, the Bible, and how has this view changed over the course of your relationship with Jesus?

_____

_____

What are some practices you use to read and study the Bible?

_____

_____

How do you feel about personalizing Scripture? Try it using one of your favorite verses:

_____

_____

Your Prayer

_____

_____

LIVING WORSHIP

> But the time is coming - indeed it's here now – when true
> worshipers will worship the Father in spirit and in truth. The Father
> is looking for those who will worship him that way.
> John 4:23

Why is worship so important to God? And what is worship anyway? Is worship the music portion of a church service? Amazingly, we could probably ask ten different people, "What is worship?" and we would more than likely get ten different answers.

Going back to the Old Testament, when the Israelites were in captivity, the Lord told Moses to go to Pharaoh and command him to let His children go so that they could worship Him. If you look closely, you can see a beautiful metaphor here. Like the Israelites, we are held captive by many things, things such as: selfishness, greed, pride or jealousy. The key to our release from these chains, from this form of bondage, is worship.

Whether we are aware of it or not, we are all worshippers. Some of us worship wealth, our kids, our spouse, success, or having some sort of recognition. Until we give that place of worship to the One we were created for, the only One Who can fill that void in our hearts and lives, we will keep searching. We will get to the end of our lives and realize, maybe when it's too late, that we have missed out on the only thing that this life is all about.

Once we make that decision to live a life of worship, how do we begin? Worship is not just singing, clapping, or raising our hands; worship is a lifestyle. I would like to point you to Matthew 22:37-38. The Pharisees and Sadducees were trying to trap Jesus by asking Him which of the commandments in the Law of Moses was most important. Listen to how Jesus responds,

> "'You must love the Lord your God with all your heart, all your soul, and all your mind.' This is the first and greatest commandment."

I believe this is the essence of worship: Loving God with all that you are, every single fiber of your being. Why? Because that is what we were created to do. God the Father literally breathed His breath into Adam, and it is that same, borrowed breath that is longing to give back its praise to Him.

God is looking for those who will worship Him "in spirit and in truth." Only then will we see Him as our Lord, our Maker, and the One who alone is worthy of our worship. To worship God is to adore Him, to love Him, and to give Him back the borrowed breath He has given us.

> *Father, show me how to worship You today. I want to love you*
> *with all my heart, all my soul, and all my mind.*

What hidden treasures did God reveal to you today? _____

_____

How would you define worship?

_____

_____

I absolutely love the phrase, "borrowed breath." In your own opinion, why can it be described as borrowed?

_____

_____

_____

Your Prayer

_____

_____

Day 6

HE IS GOOD

Surely your goodness and unfailing love will pursue me all the days of my life…
Psalm 23:6

God's Word describes many wonderful attributes about Jesus. One of those attributes happens to be His goodness, but have you ever been in a place where you have questioned that goodness? Was there a time in your life when you were so broken and things seemed like they were falling apart and you asked yourself, "Where is God in all of this?" "Is He really good?"

Having a Christian background, I would often feel guilty after asking questions like, "God, where are You?" or saying things like, "You are not Who I thought You were, God." So on top of being broken, I was dealing with guilt.

How many times do we underestimate God and the depth of His love for us? He has never been afraid of honesty. He reassured me that He is not afraid of my questions, and He reminded me that His Only Son questioned Him (Matthew 27:46). Even David, a man after God's own heart questioned Him many times. Again this morning, as I was thinking about this whole topic, I realized that John the Baptist, of whom Jesus said, "…of all who have ever lived, none is greater than John…" (Matthew 11:11) asked Jesus this question, "Are you the Messiah we've been expecting, or should we keep looking for someone else?"

So Scripture proves that Jesus does not get angry at our questions. It almost seems that He welcomes them. He wants a conversation with the real you, not some super-spiritual personification of you. Who else does He want you to take your questions to? After seeing these things, I can move past my guilt and into the heart of the matter. My original question: Is God really good, even when, from my limited perspective, it doesn't look like it?

The only reason it seems that we question God's goodness is that life or our circumstances aren't turning out as we have envisioned them. Sometimes our selfishness blinds us from seeing God for who He truly is. God wants me to surrender my life, all of it: all my dreams, all my hopes and trust that His plan is better than mine. We see only what is right in front of us while He sees the big picture, even past our lives and into eternity.

The topic of God's goodness is too vast for us to try to conquer in one day, one month or even a year, but tomorrow we will continue along this same, topic line; probing deeper into our hearts and also into the schemes of the enemy. He is the only one who could benefit from us doubting the goodness of God.

My gracious, Heavenly Father, I surrender my heart to you, my life to you. Take the veil from my eyes and let me see your goodness surrounding me today.

What hidden treasure did God reveal to you today? _____

_____

Has there ever been a time in your life that you questioned God and His goodness? If so, then get it out. What were your questions? What are still your questions?

_____

_____

_____

It is not safe to stop at your questions. Give God the opportunity to heal your brokenness. Take some time to listen to His loving voice. Write down what He reveals to you:

_____

_____

_____

Your Prayer

_____

_____

HE IS GOOD/PART 2

You are good and do only good; teach me your decrees.
Psalm 119:68

The very nature of God is goodness. He cannot help it; He is good. The scheme of the enemy is to distort our view of who God really is. That has been his plan since the very beginning. God created man because, in His goodness, He wanted a relationship with us. Then along came the Devil, disguised as a serpent, to question Eve.

"Did God really say you must not eat the fruit from any
of the trees in the garden?" (Genesis 3:1)

You see what Satan did? God had created this perfect garden, full of trees, but Satan shifts Eve's focus off of all the good trees and has her to question why God would not allow her to eat of this one tree. Satan has a strategy; he is a manipulator. He continually attacks God's character (Genesis 3:4-5).

Why should we then act surprised when Satan uses this same ploy to draw us away from the Father? We must stay focused on what Gods Word says about Him. The truth of the Scriptures need to be inscribed so deeply in our hearts that when we are tempted to question Who God is, we won't be swayed by our enemy.

Even after Adam and Eve sinned, God was still good. Their decisions didn't change God's character. Because He is a perfect God, He had to punish their sin, but because

He is also a compassionate and loving God, He had a plan in place. Two thousand years later, He took our sin punishment on Himself. His desire now is the same as it was in the garden: He longs to have a relationship with us, and the enemy is still pulling out all his tricks to keep us from that. God has always been good; He will always be good. We have a Father who is for us, who is not only good, but compassionate, faithful, trustworthy, and longing to be near you.

Oh! If we could just get a glimpse into the heart of God, how He has loved us, pursued us and longed for us! Then we would never again question His goodness.

"O Lord, you are so good, so ready to forgive, so full of unfailing love for all who ask for your help." Psalm 86:5

My loving and good Father, I bind every attack from the enemy, he is a liar. Drown out his voice in my life until all I hear is You.

What hidden treasure did God reveal to you today? _____

_____

You were created for the purpose of an intimate, personal relationship with God. What are some of the emotions and feelings that this thought evokes?

_____

_____

The enemy has power over you only if you believe what he says, only if you believe his lies. What are the lies that he has told you in an effort to keep you away from God?

_____

_____

I think it would be a great time to read today's prayer again:

My loving and good Father, I bind every attack from the enemy, he is a liar. Drown out his voice in my life until all I hear is You.

Your Prayer

_____

_____

JUST BE YOU

Because of the privilege and authority God has given me, I give each of you this warning: Don't think you are better than you really are. Be honest in your evaluation of yourselves, measuring yourselves by the faith God has given us.
Romans 12:3

I had a close friend say to me once, "You are setting a standard that no one can live up to." This totally confused me! You see, at the time she confronted me with this statement, my husband and I happened to be ministering to young adults. What I thought I was doing was trying to live a near "perfect" life that they could pattern their lives after.

However, I was guilty of making my life, my rules, and personal convictions the standard for these young adults to live by instead of pointing them to Jesus. I needed to encourage them to fall in love with Him and let Him sort out their behavior. I was, in effect, saying look at me, follow me.

What is even sadder about all of this, I myself wasn't even living the life I wanted them to think I was living. It was a façade. And the night my friend had the courage to speak truth to me, I had almost hit rock bottom. In my hypocrisy, I didn't want anyone to see my weaknesses, only my strengths. I was having health issues while also going through years of infertility; I was at an all-time low. I was questioning myself and God.

This leads me to the story of two brothers, Jacob and Esau. In this story, Jacob has lied and deceived his brother Esau, as well as his father, Isaac. Here is the abbreviated version of what has happened: Jacob pretended to be Esau and went in to his father's bedside to receive the "birthright blessing," which didn't belong to him. Because of this deception, and fearing for his very life, he runs away from home. So now, almost 20 years later, he receives a message from the Lord to return home. Jacob is on his way back to his homeland and he sends his family and all his possessions ahead of him. He is alone with God.

We pick up this story in Genesis 32:24-27

> *This left Jacob all alone in the camp, and a man came and wrestled with him until the dawn began to break. When the man saw that he would not win the match, he touched Jacob's hip and wrenched it out of its socket. Then the man said, "Let me go, for the dawn is breaking!" But Jacob said, "I will not let you go unless you bless me." "What is your name?" the man asked. He replied, "Jacob."*

If you grew up in church, this story is familiar enough to you that you just breeze right over it, but try reading it for the first time and think about it because this is a very strange story! Jacob is wrestling with God! What? What is the point of this whole story? I don't believe this was a wrestling match to see who was the strongest, but intended to see how persistent Jacob would be. Jacob wanted to be blessed, but before God blessed him, He asked him this question: "What is your name?"

God then changes Jacob's name to Israel, meaning *God Prevails.* There are so many powerful applications here, from his former name meaning *deceiver* to his new name, Israel, meaning God always is and He always wins. His purpose and His promises would be accomplished through Jacob. But before this happened, God asked Jacob his name. How interesting. Didn't God know who Jacob was? It is my belief that God wanted Jacob to see, to admit, who he really was, to take off the mask and stop pretending to be someone he was not. "What is your name?"

God the Father is asking us this same question: "What is your name? Who are you, really? Not the person you want everyone to see, but the real you." That is the person God can minister to and the person God will use to minster through.

No matter the name you think you have, He calls you chosen (1 Peter 3:9); you are His child (John 1:12); He does not condemn you (Romans 8:1), but He accepts you, the true you (Romans 15:7), and He calls you blameless (Ephesians 1:4).

What frightens the enemies of God is for believers to know their true name, to rise up to the calling placed on their lives, and to be vulnerable enough to let others see their weaknesses, not just their strengths. If we are honest about our identity; if we come face to face with who we are, God will meet us there, ready and willing to take our hand as He whispers, "I knew who you were all along; I have been waiting on you."

I am sure we have all heard the saying, "People relate to your struggles more than they do your strengths," and the more time passes, the more I realize the simple truth in that. Let us all be willing to take our mask off and unveil our hearts to a world that is desperately searching for authenticity.

Father, who am I? Who have I hidden from everyone, including You? Call me forth as You minister to me and through me.

What hidden treasure did God reveal to you today? _____

_____

Who are you? What is your personality, your likes and dislikes?

_____

_____

_____

Are you guilty of wearing a mask, allowing others to only see your strengths?

_____

_____

_____

God loves you, yes you! You were created *on* purpose *for* a purpose! Take time in your prayer today to thank Him for who you are in Him.

Your Prayer

_____

_____

CAN I TRUST HIM

Trust in the Lord with all your heart; do not depend on your own understanding.
Proverbs 3:5

Ah, my life verse. It is amazing over the years how many times I have repeated this verse to myself. Sometimes in a frustrated tone, "Trust in the Lord." Sometimes in tears, I cry those same words, "Trust in the Lord." No matter the season I may find myself in, those words safeguard my life.

I am of the opinion that faith and trust go hand in hand. Both faith and trust place the responsibility on someone else's shoulders. When I choose not to trust God, in effect, I am choosing to trust myself. If my faith is not in God, it is in something else or someone else.

I have come to this conclusion: My heart and my life are the safest when in the hands of the One who made them; in the hands of the One who knows me better than I know myself. The second half of Proverbs 3:5 says that I cannot depend on my own understanding. Why? Because I only see small parts of this life, not just my life, but the lives around me. My Father sees all, He knows all, and He understands all.

I believe Proverbs 3:6 wraps up the full thoughts of verse five. "Seek his will in all you do, and he will show you which path to take." When life starts throwing me curveballs, God's Word says that all I need to do is seek His will, and He will show me what to do and where to go. He is just asking me to trust Him. To be able to fully trust someone, you have to know that person.

This hasn't always been my life verse, mainly because I didn't trust the Lord with all my heart. My lack of trust was because I didn't know Him. When I understand His character, that He is good, has always been good, will always be good, that He is perfect, that He is incapable of making a mistake, that He delights in me, that He rejoices over me, I can trust Him because I know Him. I can trust Him because there will never be anyone who will love me like He does. There will never be anyone who pursues me like He will. He only has my best interest at heart. He is worthy of my trust, worthy of me completely putting "all my heart" in His hands.

> *Father, are there any areas in my life that I am not putting my complete trust in You? Guide me as I learn to put all of my hopes, all of my dreams and all of my faith into Your perfect, loving hands.*

What hidden treasure did God reveal to you today? _____

_____

On a scale of 1 to 10, with 1 being very little and 10 being completely, how would you honestly evaluate the way you currently trust in God. Explain your self-evaluation:

_____

_____

_____

Would you say that your lack of trust in God is stemming from not knowing Him intimately or is your lack of trust based on something else?

_____

_____

Are you at a place in your life that you can say that you are ready to put all your faith, all your hopes, and all your dreams into God's hands and trust Him? How did you get to this point or what will it take for you to get to this point?

_____

_____

Your Prayer

_____

_____

CAN I HAVE A WITNESS

But you will receive power when the Holy Spirit comes upon you. And you
will be my witnesses, telling people about me everywhere – in Jerusalem,
throughout Judea, in Samaria, and to the ends of the earth.
Acts 1:8

I used to think one of the scariest things about being a Christian was having to witness
to people. Yes, I really did just say that. Please tell me I am not the only one!

I am just speaking for myself here, but for many years, this is how it played out (in my
mind of course). I see the unsuspecting stranger in line at the grocery store, or maybe it is
a relative at a family reunion, or perhaps even a waiter at my favorite restaurant. My heart
starts pounding; I am trying to figure out if the Lord is nudging me to say something or
is it just me feeling condemned if I don't? Oh man, the struggle is real! What do I say?
Maybe I should ease into it by asking the famous, "Where do you go to church" question
because that seems to work well here in the South.

I cannot tell you how many times this has happened to me; it was an endless cycle!

Here in the book of Acts, we have the account of Jesus ascending to heaven, but before
He goes, He leaves the disciples with this message: "…be my witnesses." The definition
of a witness is "a person who sees an event take place," and "to give or serve as evidence
of; testify to."

Hmmm…let's just think about this for a minute. What exactly is Jesus telling the disciples to do; what is He asking them to say? My personal assessment is this: before ascending into heaven, Jesus basically gives the disciples their own personal script. He is asking them to tell other people what they themselves have seen, what they have experienced and felt.

Now this is getting interesting!

Do you know how you can connect with a stranger, a friend, coworker or relative? Be authentic. Be real. Connect with someone by being vulnerable and sharing what God has personally done in your life. Witnessing was hard because I made witnessing about me. Jesus said in John 12:32:

> "And when I am lifted up from the earth, I will draw everyone to myself."

If you are a Believer in Jesus Christ, then our job is to lift up the name of Jesus, through the way we live, through the testimony of our lives, through sharing what He has done in us and what He has done for us. After that, we leave the rest up to Him. Just like His command to the disciples, Jesus is asking us to tell other people what we ourselves have seen, experienced, and felt.

Father, help me to take the pressure off of myself and place it on You.
Show me and teach me how to be an effective witness wherever I may go
today, I pray that I will live in such a way that lifts up Your Name.

What hidden treasure did God reveal to you today? _____

_____

What is your past experience with witnessing to others?

_____

_____

By definition, what is a witness?

_____

Allowing others to see Jesus in our lives takes vulnerability and transparency. What has God done in your life that you could share with someone today?

_____

_____

_____

Your Prayer

_____

_____

MERCY

So it is God who decides to show mercy. We can neither choose it nor work for it.
Romans 9:16

One of the things that ranks high in my list of "spiritual priorities" for the health of my soul is personal worship time. It may sound strange at first, but I have found it to be what gives me strength, changes my attitude, and focuses my perspective.

During one of these intimate times with my Father, as I was pouring out myself to Him, I spoke these words: "All I am is Yours." In that moment, while I was waiting in His presence, I heard Him respond almost immediately, repeating my words back to me, "All I am is Yours." It took me by surprise. Did I hear that correctly? "Yes, Brooke, All I am is yours. All my strength, all my peace, even my very Spirit is yours."

Can you even grasp this? That the God of all creation, of all mankind telling us that all He is can be ours. What type of God is this? Certainly not One that I thought I knew. I have felt for years that I was just attempting to live in a way to appease Him, to stay on His "good side." But listen to this exclamation in Micah 7:18

> "Where is another God like you, who pardons the guilt of the remnant, overlooking the sins of his special people?", then my favorite part, "because you delight in showing unfailing love."

> Another version says it this way: "He delights in mercy." NKJV

He desires to have compassion on us and to show us His mercy. His Word is full of this love story; the story of God pursuing us at all cost. Do you know why He can look past our sins, as referred to in Micah chapter seven? When He took our place on the cross and we accepted His life and death as payment for our sins, He no longer can see that sin. His righteousness becomes my righteousness:

"Yet God, with undeserved kindness, declares that we are righteous." (Romans 3:24)

I deserved nothing, yet He gave me everything! So yes, All He is, is mine!

He wipes our slate clean every morning (Lamentations 3:23), He rejoices over us with singing, taking delight in us with gladness (Zephaniah 3:17). He is not an angry Father, but a merciful Father, in pursuit of our hearts, willing and ready to give us all of Himself.

Father, all I am is Yours. Come make your home in my heart.

What hidden treasure did God reveal to you today? _____

_____

Has there been a time that you can recall where God has spoken to you? Write down this experience:

_____

_____

How does it make you feel to hear that God pursued you at all cost?

_____

_____

Were you able to sincerely pray the prayer at the end of the devotional today? Why or Why not?

_____

_____

Your Prayer

_____

_____

LOVING WELL

Your love for one another will prove to the world that you are my disciples.
John 13:35

When I was growing up, we had these cassette tapes called "Mr. Donut Man." These cassette tapes had children's songs on them and each tape would also have a Scripture verse. When it came time to learn the verse, Mr. Donut Man would present the verse with a tempo and word pattern for the sake of memorization. Then he would invite all these children to sing along and put Bible to memory. It really made rides to school fun!

Today's verse from the book of John brings all those childhood memories back because this is one of the verses Mr. Donut Man helped me memorize! After all these years, I can still remember the tune.

The principle of this verse is so much deeper than I realized when I was seven or eight years old. When I put this verse to memory, I actually learned it in the King James Version, which says,

"By this shall all men know that ye are my disciples, if ye have love one to another."

These verses are red in the Bible because they are words that Jesus spoke.

Picture this: It is the Passover night. Jesus has finished washing His disciples' feet in an act of servant leadership. Judas has just left the room for the purpose of betraying Jesus and turning Him over to the religious authorities. With all of this in mind, Jesus then starts a conversation with His disciples, trying to prepare them for what is about to happen-his betrayal and crucifixion. The last thing you would think Jesus was going to say was something on love.

> "So now I am giving you a new commandment: Love each other. Just as I have loved you, you should love each other." John 13:34

This one little phrase jumps off the page at me: "Just as I have loved you." How did Jesus love His disciples? He loved them at all cost. He loved them unconditionally, even while being betrayed, denied, and abandoned. In essence He is saying, "See how I have loved you; now, you go and love like that. This is how the world will know that you belong to Me, by how well you love."

On one of the darkest days in His life, as Jesus is being betrayed, He says to His followers, "Love each other." This makes me wonder: who can I not love? As a follower of Christ, I have no sensible reason to hold a grudge or un-forgiveness in my heart towards anyone. My love is to represent the love of Jesus: unconditional love - love without limitations or conditions - and love given freely to anyone and everyone.

> *Father, I want to love like You love. I want the world to know You just by looking at me. Help me as I learn to be a reflection of You.*

What hidden treasure did God reveal to you today? _____

_____

What does it tell you about Jesus' character that in the moments of betrayal He was giving His disciples a lesson on how to love well?

_____

_____

Have you experienced unconditional love?

_____

_____

How well do you love? Could your love be described as unconditional, without stipulations, and freely given to anyone?

_____

_____

Your Prayer

_____

_____

LET'S DANCE

For the Lord your God is living among you. He is a mighty Savior.
He will take delight in you with gladness. With his love, he will calm
all your fears. He will rejoice over you with joyful songs.
Zephaniah 3:17

I can remember the day I first heard this verse. It absolutely threw me for a loop! Why? It was a view of God that I have never had:

For the Lord your God is living among you. Okay, got that, God the Creator is living in the midst of His creation.

He is a mighty savior. Yes, He sure is! He is magnificent beyond words!

He will take delight in you with gladness. What? Delight in me? Hmmm, well okay, but for the most part, I thought He just "endured me." The fact that He delights in me is going to have to change how I view Him, but it doesn't stop there:

With his love, he will calm all your fears. I used to be a very, and I mean very, fearful person. I feared sicknesses, I feared people, I feared being alone or being lonely. According to this verse, guess what the solution is - God's love. He calms all my fears with His love. This next phrase is my favorite…

He will rejoice over you with joyful songs. "God, You rejoice over me with singing?" In this verse, the phrase "rejoice over you" literally means "dance, skip, leap, and spin around in joy." It is hard for me to wrap my mind around a God who spins around wildly at the thoughts of me.

Singer and song writer, Dennis Jernigan, said this: "I don't get to decide if God loves me. I have two choices; Do I accept this love or do I reject it? If He rejoices over me, then I embrace that." Listen to the words of the song Dennis wrote after this revelation from Zephaniah 3:17

"When the night is falling, and the day is done, I can hear you calling, "Come." I will come, while you sing over me. When the night surrounds me, all my dreams undone, I can hear you calling, "Come." I will come, while You sing over me. When the night would hide my way…I will listen until I hear You say, How I love you child, I love you! How I love you, child I love you! How I love you!"

My old view of God couldn't allow me to see myself loved like this. Does He just tolerate me, or does He spin around wildly at the thought of me? Is He frustrated at everything I'm fearful of, or does He calm my fears with His perfect, all consuming love?

Do I adjust God's Word to better fit me and my opinion, or do I change my view of God to conform and transform my heart and my life to what His Word says about His love for me?

This kind of love pursues me; it surrounds me and envelops every aspect of my life. As I now read this verse, I throw myself fully into the arms of my Father, and what once was a dance for One, has now become our dance together.

My dear Father, what does your voice sound like as You sing over me? Help me not to fear intimacy with You but to embrace You completely, as you take delight in me, your child.

What hidden treasure did God reveal to you today? _____

_____

"He will take delight in you with gladness." God delights in you. Take a moment to let that thought soak in and reflect on what this means to you.

_____

_____

God rejoices over you with singing and dancing! What do you imagine this looks like?

_____

_____

Your Prayer

_____

_____

Day 14

MISTAKEN IDENTITY

But you are not like that, for you are a chosen people. You are royal priests, a holy nation, God's very own possession. As a result, you can show others the goodness of God, for He called you out of the darkness into his wonderful light.
I Peter 2:9

Have you ever asked yourself the question, "Who am I?" I certainly have. We can find our identity, or should I say, lose our identity, in so many different ways: focusing on careers, being a wife, a parent, or even being in ministry. While all these things can certainly be part of our calling, none of them are supposed to be our identity.

Peter, one of the twelve disciples, was formerly called Simon. From reading about Peter in the Gospels, I think we could conclude that at times, even Peter wondered about his true identity. Peter was loud and boisterous, quick-tempered and impulsive, saying and doing things without much thought. However, Jesus chose him anyway and spoke directly into his future identity, calling Peter, the "Rock" (Matthew 16:18)

Knowing his story and his background, helps me appreciate what Peter wrote in this verse from first Peter 2 which states, that just as Jesus chose Peter, He chose you too. As His child, He then calls you royalty, holy, and His very own possession. This is your identity. You are loved, so loved that God the Father chose you. No matter how you may see yourself at this very moment, God calls you blameless, innocent, and without fault.

"Yet now he has reconciled you to himself through the death of Christ in his physical body. As a result, he has brought you into his own presence, and you are holy and blameless as you stand before him without a single fault. Colossians 1:22

No matter what this world has called you or what your family or friends have called you, as a child of the most High God, His opinion is the only one that matters.

Father, help me to see my true identity. I am amazed at the lengths You have gone to, to draw me to Yourself, show me who I am in You today.

What hidden treasure did God reveal to you today? _____

_____

Do you feel as though your identity has been wrapped up in a job title, ministry, or as a parent? Why would God want you to first be identified as His child before anything else?

_____

_____

Jesus called Peter "the Rock," speaking Peter's identity over him. He was speaking into who Peter was going to become. Who is Jesus calling you to become?

_____

_____

Your Prayer

_____

_____

SO CLOSE

The Lord himself watches over you! The Lord stands
beside you as your protective shade.
Psalm 121:5

Every fall before school started back, my parents would take us to the mountains for a day-trip. I always looked forward to this trip because we would get to spend all day with my dad's undivided attention. Away from his job, yard work, and the stress that came along with it, dad gave his full attention to us girls. I could actually feel his delight in me.

That is the feeling I get as I read this verse from Psalms. The Lord is taking two postures in this one verse: beside me and over me. The psalmist says that the Lord is 'over' me so He can watch me. Now some people view the idea of God watching them constantly as a threat or something to be scared of, almost like God is watching and waiting for them to "mess up." Does that sound like God's character as you read these verses:

The Lord is compassionate and merciful, slow to get angry
and filled with unfailing love. Psalm 103:8

But you, O Lord, are a God of compassion and mercy, slow to get angry
and filled with unfailing love and faithfulness. Psalm 86:15

He watches us because we are His children and He delights in us. If you haven't yet decided to give your life to Him, if you do not identify yourself as a "child of God," He is calling to you, wooing you to Himself. Jeremiah 31:3 says that He has loved you with an everlasting love and with unfailing love, He has drawn you to Himself.

The second part of Psalm 121:5 says, "the Lord stands beside you as a protective shade." 'Beside' is the second posture God is taking in this one verse. Now the feminine side of me loves the idea of being protected. To protect something means that you have to value it. God values me. I am of the highest value and importance to Him. He cares about me, my well-being; every little detail of my life matters to my Father. Just look at where He is while protecting me: right beside me. So close beside me that I am actually in His shade. Now that is close!

> *Oh Father, thank You, simply thank You. I matter to You, You value me, You protect me and guard me. Thank You.*

What hidden treasure did God reveal to you today? _____

_____

What does it mean to you to know that God is watching you?

_____

_____

Every detail of your life matters to God. Knowing this, what are some of the areas in your life that you would like to invite Him into?

_____

_____

_____

Are you at a place in your relationship with God that you feel the closeness that was described in today's study? Would you like to be identified as a "child of God?" If so, take a moment to invite Him into your life.

_____

_____

Your Prayer

_____

_____

DECISIONS, DECISIONS

This is what the Lord says – your Redeemer, the Holy One of
Israel: "I am the Lord your God, who teaches you what is good
for you and leads you along the paths you should follow."
Isaiah 48:17

I just finished washing grapes and also making a batch of chocolate oatmeal cookies. As I popped a grape in my mouth, I stared at those warm, gooey oatmeal cookies. So I did what any normal human being would do, I swallowed that grape as fast as I could then licked the remaining batter from the oatmeal cookie bowl!

After I saw how weak my will-power was, it made me think about all the choices we are faced with in a single day. From the time I wake up and decide to drink coffee until the moment I go to bed and decide which side to sleep on, there is no telling how many decisions I will face in just a single day!

While the examples I gave are very small in the grand scheme of life or even a single day, my point is this: our choices matter. Some of our choices not only affect our life, but the lives of those around us: our family members, friends, and sometimes even strangers.

What if God put it on my heart to go pray for someone, or maybe encourage another. What if He even asked me to pay for a stranger's meal or groceries? You see, my obedience to all these choices doesn't just affect me anymore. What alarms me is this: Am I affecting more people with my obedience or my disobedience?

If you are like me, you would rather hurt yourself before you hurt anyone else. The idea of me hurting someone because I was too timid, too busy, or too shy seems very selfish. I have the opportunity every day to show others the beautiful heart of my Father.

It should be our deepest desire to bring our Father glory, to point others to Him; not to point out how good we are, but to show others how good He is. I want to be obedient when He speaks to me. If He is on the lookout for someone to send, someone to represent Him, I want to be the one He calls on. The best way I have found to learn how to hear His voice is to spend time with Him, to talk to Him as I would my best friend and then give Him a chance to speak back. According to our verse today, He said He would teach you.

Father, who can I minister to today? Open my eyes to see what You see and open my heart to feel what you feel. I choose to live this day for You.

What hidden treasure did God reveal to you today? _____

_____

Can you see how our choices affect more than just ourselves? Did any specific decision or choice you have made come to mind as you read this?

_____

_____

Would you be brave enough to ask yourself this question: "Am I affecting more people with my obedience or my disobedience?"

_____

_____

Your Prayer

_____

_____

GENTLENESS

But the Holy Spirit produces this kind of fruit in our lives: love,
joy, peace, patience, kindness, goodness, faithfulness, gentleness,
and self-control. There is no law against these things!
Galatians 5:22-23

These nine attributes are more commonly referred to as the "Fruit of the Spirit." They are nine characteristics that should be evident in a person or community living in accord with the Holy Spirit. Words like love, joy, and peace give us all the warm fuzzy feelings. Then words like patience, kindness, and goodness follow right behind. Rounding up this dynamic list are faithfulness, gentleness, and self-control.

As I was sitting outside yesterday, I was asking God to reveal Himself to a group of ladies that I am leading in a Bible study. I prayed these words: "God, show them who You are." Now I was not expecting a reply, but reply He did! He said this: "Brooke, you show them who I am."

I had never felt so incapable or inadequate as I did in that moment. Why would He give me such a task? "Oh God, can I do that?"

That is when the "Fruit of the Spirit" came to mind. It was like I wanted a checklist to see how I was doing in this mandate to represent God. Now while I am very far from perfect, and I know I need more help from my Father for all of these gifts, one in particular stood out to me. It actually made me wonder: How many times had I overlooked gentleness as a fruit of the Spirit?

For me to gain a better understanding of this word, I needed to look up synonyms for "gentle." Here are a few: kind, tender, sympathetic, considerate, understanding, compassionate. As I look at this list, it breaks my heart to think that I probably could not use any of those words to describe myself.

Why would God, in a moment when I was completely honest with Him, speak this one word to me – 'gentleness?' Quite honestly, this was my Father being a gentle Teacher. He did not come across harshly and criticize me on what a terrible job I was doing representing Him or tell me I blew it that morning getting agitated at my spouse. He was **gently** coming to me, **gently** reminding me of my call to show the world who He is.

Father, You are perfect Love, constant Joy and overwhelming Peace. You are always Patient and Kind and Good. You are the faithful One and You are my gentle Teacher. Will You come and teach me how to be more like You?

What hidden treasure did God reveal to you today? _____

_____

Out of the nine attributes of the "Fruit of the Spirit," which one stands out the most to you? Take that one trait and elaborate on what that word means.

_____

_____

_____

Your Prayer

_____

_____

ENOUGH

So don't be afraid; you are more valuable to God than a whole flock of sparrows.
Matthew 10:31

Remember what I said on Day 11, that I was praying to my Father one day, and as I told Him "all I am is Yours," He repeated those words back to me, "All I am is yours." Well guess what, it happened again, as I said something to Him, He repeated the very same words back to me!

Here is what happened: Two nights ago, it was actually a Sunday night, and as I was thinking and mentally preparing for the week ahead, the feeling of inadequacy seemed to engulf me. I suddenly felt incapable of leading a group of ladies in Bible study the following night, incapable of mentoring and discipling a different group of ladies. I felt like a failure in my relationships and also a failure as a wife. In a moment, I felt so far from who I needed to be and also who I wanted to be.

Then that familiar voice, the voice that my soul was created to hear, began to speak over me. "I need you to calmly trust Me. Be at peace because I am enough. I can defend you, sustain you, and carry you. I want you to stop putting so much pressure on yourself to be perfect; I have never required perfection from you. Love Me, set your gaze upon Me. Stop focusing on circumstances; stop focusing on yourself and your inadequacy, and stop getting sidetracked by people's opinion of you. Simply love Me."

Oh, how His words can pierce the deepest needs and pains of my heart. As I sat in silence, reflecting on what He had just revealed to me, I began to say to Him, "You are enough,

You are enough, You are enough." That is when He repeated those words over me, "You are enough, you are enough, you are enough."

As what He was saying was sinking in, I began to question it, "Am I enough, really?" But if the God of all creation, of all mankind says I am, then I am. And He says those same words over you today as well, "You are enough." No matter what you may feel, no matter what has happened to you, and no matter what this next week, next month or next year may look like, you are enough!

How do I know this? Because God's power is at work within us.

Look at Ephesians 1:19-23

I also pray that you will understand the incredible greatness of God's power for us who believe him. This is the same mighty power that raised Christ from the dead and seated him in the place of honor at God's right hand in the heavenly realms. Now he is far above any ruler or authority or power or leader or anything else - not only in this world but also in the world to come. God has put all things under the authority of Christ and has made him head over all things for the benefit of the church. And the church is his body; it is made full and complete by Christ, who fills all things everywhere with himself.

That last verse says that Christ has filled all things with Himself. I am enough, you are enough, why? Because He is in us and He is always enough.

So that feeling of not measuring up, that feeling of inadequacy cannot be from our loving Father. If He cared for us enough to fill us with Himself, He would never say those things. We need to know how to spot an attack from the enemy. The enemy comes to "steal, kill and destroy," but God has come to give you "a rich and satisfying life" (John 10:10).

*Father, reveal to me today my value. I know that You are
enough, but please show me today that I am enough.*

What hidden treasure did God reveal to you today? _____

_____

What currently has you feeling overwhelmed, insufficient, and inadequate?

_____

_____

_____

Do you feel like you are "enough?"

_____

_____

Ephesians 1:19-23 speaks of God's mighty power and how He fills all things with Himself. Personalize this passage in order to know how God wants to fill you with Himself, enabling you to become more than enough.

_____

_____

_____

Your Prayer

_____

_____

THE HURDLE

"The Lord delights in his people:..."
Psalm 149:4a

I am in the middle of preparing to share my testimony at a church in our community. While I find it very humbling to think that I would be asked to stand before a congregation, this privilege comes with a great responsibility, because I want to represent my Father well. I want to convey to a group of strangers what it was like to be broken, lonely, and afraid and to now be free from all of that.

As I sat pondering all of this, I asked the question, "What took me so long to work out this relationship with You, Lord? What was my stumbling block?" I knew if I could figure this out, then maybe, just maybe, I could help others jump this hurdle sooner and quicker than the years it took me.

Over the next few days, God began showing me that while I was going through the difficult seasons of infertility, the reason I questioned Him, the reason I became angry at Him was all because of a lack of trust in Him. It ultimately boiled down to one little, or should I say, big reason: I did not know how much I was loved by my Heavenly Father. I could not fully trust Him because I did not really know Him. Oh yes, I grew up in church, attended a Christian School, and knew all about God in my head, but not in my heart.

John 3:16 is one of those verses that most people, especially Believers, know from memory,

> "For this is how God loved the world: He gave his one and only Son, so that everyone who believes in Him will not perish but have eternal life."

Of course, I knew God loved the world, but did I know that God loved me? Actually, to be honest, as I stated before, I thought God at most, tolerated me. I felt that He was looking at me in a perpetual state of disappointment; If only I knew, really knew, how deep His love is, how passionate He is for me and how much He delights and enjoys me (yes me and yes, you too!) Knowing this simple, yet profound truth, will shift your perspective of your life and your life circumstances.

When you can grasp the fact that you are so deeply loved, that you are continually pursued, and that the God of all creation delights in you, you will find it easy to trust Him.

If like me, you find yourself in a situation where you feel helpless, spiritually discouraged, and even abandoned, maybe the solution is to find some time to get alone with your Father and allow Him to speak His love over you. His love for you is unconditional; it has nothing to do with who you are, but everything to do with who He is.

> *Father, I take comfort in Your unfailing and unconditional love for me today. Help me to fully grasp that You are a God that can be trusted.*

What hidden treasure did God reveal to you today? _____

_____

What seems to be your own personal hurdle into a more consistent and more intimate relationship with God?

_____

_____

Our lack of trust in God seems to lead us in to questioning Him. What are some of those areas where you feel that you have the most questions/lack of trust?

_____

_____

Knowing how deeply you are loved will transform your entire view of your life and your level of trust. Ask God to cover up all your doubts and all your questions within His unconditional love for you.

Your Prayer

_____

_____

Day 20

IT'S TIME TO DREAM AGAIN

*Now all glory to God, who is able, through his mighty power at work
within us, to accomplish infinitely more that we might ask or think.*
Ephesians 3:20

This verse is amazing! It happens to be a verse I have known for a long time, but only in the last few months did it move from my head to my heart. I was challenged to not just quote that verse for other people as a source of encouragement, but to also proclaim it over my own life. Could I really believe what this verse says? That God can do more than I could even ask or think?

Rick Warren wrote this about Ephesians 3:20: "First, you dare to ask for it. If you want God's blessings on your life this year, you must dare to ask for it. 'God, what's your dream for my life? What do You want me to do?' Then ask yourself, "What would I attempt for God if I knew I couldn't fail?"

This revelation gives you a whole new perspective on life, on faith, and also on the dreams held in your heart. Guess who put those dreams there? Guess who made you with your own, individual personality, your little quirks and traits that set you apart from everyone else? Those things that we have come to believe about ourselves that make us 'different' are the things that in reality set us apart. There has never been nor will there ever be anyone like you.

God created me and God created you for a specific time, a specific purpose, and He has placed a dream in your heart that He is now calling forth. No more being scared and timid. No more waiting. No more can we allow the lies of the enemy to discourage or distract us from being all that God has called us to be. Why not let today be the day that your faith and your dreams collide.

While taking a few moments to allow God to speak to you and as you give Him the freedom into those deep desires and hopes that are in your heart, I want to leave you with this verse:

> "I am the LORD, the God of all the peoples of the world.
> Is anything too hard for me?" Jeremiah 32:27

> *Father, show me how to dream again. What are You calling me to do? Place a God-sized dream inside me.*

What hidden treasure did God reveal to you today? _____

_____

What is that dream held in your heart, so big that only God can make it happen?

_____

_____

_____

Personalize the Scripture from Ephesians 3:20 and Jeremiah 32:27

_____

_____

_____

_____

Your Prayer

_____

_____

CONSISTENCY

Jesus Christ is the same yesterday, today, and forever.
Hebrews 13:8

Consistency. Now that's a word you don't use every day. I wonder if that is because consistency is such a rare quality or attribute? I mean, when is the last time that you used that word to describe anyone? Many times, my physical life as well as my spiritual life seem so far from consistent, that I now believe this word, this way of life, is unattainable.

For instance, one day this week I felt so loved by my Heavenly Father, so assured of our relationship; then in less than twenty-four hours, after hearing some drastic news about a family member's health, I felt overwhelmed. Guess what, twenty-four hours later I was having to tell myself to pray because I didn't feel like it! How can we feel this rollercoaster of emotions in just a week's time? And in some cases, in a single day?

I believe one of the reasons is that we let our external lives intrude into our internal lives. No matter what may be going on around us, when we are in a constant relationship with the Father, we can be internally at rest, at peace, knowing some simple, basic truths:

> **God is for us**. "What shall we say about such wonderful things as these?
> If God is for us, who can ever be against us?" Romans 8:31 **God is good**.
> "Praise the LORD! Give thanks to the LORD, for he is good! His faithful
> love endures forever." Psalm 106:1 **God is consistent**. "Whatever is good and

perfect comes down to us from God our Father, who created all the lights in the heavens. He never changes or casts a shifting shadow." James 1:17

I love the last part of that verse from James, "He never changes." How comforting to know that despite my emotions and how I may be feeling today, God will not change. He is the same yesterday as He will be today and tomorrow. His love for us is constant. His approval and affection for us is enough to get us through the best of days and the worst of days.

To live an effective Christian life, we must be rooted and grounded in Him. His consistency becomes our consistency.

Father, Your faithfulness amazes me. Keep me rooted and grounded in You; I want to lead a life of consistency.

What hidden treasure did God reveal to you today? _____

_____

Looking back over your last week, could you say that your emotional, physical, and spiritual life could be described as "consistent?" Why or why not?

_____

_____

Why is it not safe to always trust our emotions?

_____

_____

_____

How do we stay "rooted and grounded" in Christ? (Colossians 2:6-7)

_____

_____

Your Prayer

_____

_____

THE LETTER

For this is how God loved the world: He gave his one and only Son, so that everyone who believes in him will not perish but have eternal life. God sent his Son into the world not to judge the world, but to save the world through him.
John 3:16-17

A couple of years ago I was challenged to write a letter to myself from God. What would God say to me? More importantly, what would God say to you? If you went to your mailbox today, opened a letter addressed to you, with the sender's name, "Your Heavenly Father," what would you expect that letter to say when you opened it?

Before I challenge you to start your own letter, may I go ahead and give you a couple of guidelines?

1. He does not condemn you: According to today's Scripture in John 3:16-17, God loves you so much that He has placed all of your guilt, all of your sins, all condemnation, on the back of His Son, Jesus. God did not send Jesus to judge you. Jesus has come to demonstrate how much God the Father loves you.

2. He Understands You: Oh yes, even those things you don't let anyone else see. Not only does He see you, He "gets" you, the real you. "Nothing in all creation is hidden from God. Everything is naked and exposed before his eyes, and he is the one to whom we are accountable." Hebrews 4:13

3. He Wants to Talk to You: This single fact blows me away. God wants to talk to you! Our problem is that we either don't take the time to listen or we are afraid if we do, we might not like what He would say. Oh, how I wish you could hear the Father's heart for you. He loves you, magnificently loves you!

> "See how very much our Father loves us, for he calls us his
> children, and that is what we are!..." I John 3:1

Okay, so here is the challenge: ask God to speak to you. Give Him the freedom into your heart, into your life. In view of His great love for you, what is He saying to you today? Now take a deep breath, and begin…

Father, show me your heart for me. What do you want to say to me?

_____

_____

_____

_____

_____

_____

_____

_____

_____

_____

RECEIVE IT

I am leaving you with a gift – peace of mind and heart. And the peace I
give is a gift the world cannot give. So don't be troubled or afraid.
John 14:27

Who doesn't love to receive gifts? Especially a gift that comes for no particular reason other than the generosity of the giver. That is exactly what is happening in our Scripture text today. Jesus' time on earth is coming to an end (unbeknownst to the disciples), and Jesus is trying to prepare them by letting them all know that when He leaves, He is leaving them with a gift…peace. Listen to how Eugene Peterson puts it in the Message translation:

"I'm leaving you well and whole. That's my parting gift to you.
Peace. I don't leave you the way you're used to being left – feeling
abandoned, bereft. So don't be upset. Don't be distraught."

Peace: the freedom from disturbance. Is that a characterization of your life? If this is a gift that is still being offered by Jesus, how can we receive it? How can our life reflect a life at peace? I have some wonderful news. The same peace Jesus offered His disciples is the same peace He continues to offer us today.

Who wouldn't want peace of mind and heart, a peace that no one, or no thing, can take away? A peace that no matter what is happening all around me or happening to me, my heart and my mind are free from disturbance. How can this be, and is this even possible?

Jesus goes on to say, "…the peace I give…the world cannot give." There is our answer. The world cannot take it away because the world did not give it to you.

I am passionate about this peace because I have personally experienced it. My hope for you today is for you to experience it as well. Here is the whole principle on a life of peace: you have to receive a gift. Jesus is offering you this same gift He offered to His disciples, peace of mind and heart. It is yours, freely, just receive it.

Father, I not only want Your peace, I need Your peace. I have tried to do things my way, going after what I thought would give me peace, but I have failed. I want You. I need You. Come make Your place in my heart and bring me internal peace and eternal peace.

What hidden treasure did God reveal to you today? _____

_____

Why do you think Jesus referred to His peace as a gift?

_____

_____

Have you attempted to find peace on your own, apart from God? Why did it not work or not last?

_____

_____

What are some of the personal benefits you could experience from having the lasting peace that God is offering you?

_____

_____

Your Prayer

_____

_____

JUMP IN

O that we might know the Lord! Let us press on to know Him. He will respond
to us as surely as the arrival of dawn or the coming of rains in early spring.
Hosea 6:3

You don't know what hot is until you have experienced a humid July day in the piedmont
of North Carolina. It is like being in an oven and a sauna at the same time! Thankfully,
I have a pool within steps of my house. However, I have yet to get in my pool this year.
I can look at the pool, appreciate having a pool, but never fully enjoy all the benefits of
the pool unless I get in it!

As I was thinking about this last week, I realized that this is how many people view
God. They know He is there, appreciate having Him close, but never engage into a
relationship with Him. I understand that there could be many reasons for this, but the
two that seem most common are a wrong view of who God is or a lack of understanding
what a relationship with God is supposed to look like.

Hopefully by now, on day twenty-four of your SEARCHING journey, you are starting
to understand how trustworthy and how good our Father God is. His love is deep, His
love is consistent, and His love is not based on your performance. He is passionately in
love with you and is waiting expectantly for your returned affection.

Or maybe you find yourself where I was, ready to engage in this relationship but not
knowing where to start or how to begin? Quite honestly and directly, it is as simple as

me going to my pool and jumping in! God's Word says that He knows our hearts. He knows when you are wanting to know Him more; He sees you as you read and pray, as You hunger for more of Him, He hears those cries of your heart for intimacy, and He is waiting for your invitation.

The last part of Hosea 6:3 says that "He will respond to us as surely as the arrival of dawn." As sure as we know that the sun will rise in the morning is as sure as you can be that He will respond to your invitation. He has been waiting for you your whole life.

Father, come. Come and make your home in me and with me. I want a relationship with You. I want to be your best friend. Thank You for Your patience with me and for waiting on my heart to turn to You.

What hidden treasure did God reveal to you today? _____

_____

How would you describe God's unconditional love for you?

_____

_____

Are you seeking a deeper relationship with God but unsure of the next steps? Write down your thoughts on the subject of knowing God in a deeper, more intimate way:

_____

_____

_____

Personalize todays passage from Hosea 6:3

_____

_____

Your Prayer

_____

_____

HOME

For this world is not our permanent home; We are looking for a home yet to come.
Hebrews 13:14

I absolutely love vacation! The whole process of going on a trip is exciting to me: the planning, the anticipation, the actual destination; I love it all! However, when you are on vacation, you know that it will eventually come to an end. Maybe that is why we sometimes never fully unpack our bags or get settled into our hotel room or condo.

Look at our verse for the day from Hebrews. Just as we know we are not home while on vacation, we need to also know that this world is not our permanent home. God wants us to be conscious of our eternal life and live with expectancy for a future home. We are told in Colossians 3 to "set our sights on heaven" and "to think about the things of heaven." Why would God want us to think so much about heaven while we live here on earth? As a result of keeping our sights on heaven, we live differently; we live with a new-found purpose.

According to John 10:10, I believe we are meant to live life to the fullest; and while we enjoy people and animals and creation, we should also live with an understanding that we are just passing through, like tourists: enjoying all the sights, the beauty, our fellow travelers, the splendor of it all. But knowing down deep in our hearts that we won't live here forever shifts our focus heavenward.

I like to call this an Eternity Mindset, a mindset that changes how we love, how we give, and how we view our own life. It is easy to let our daily lives distract us from focusing on our citizenship in heaven. We can find ourselves getting caught up in the rat-race of life, the mentality of looking out for ourselves, but God desires something different for His children. His desire for His children is for us to live a life knowing our Father is preparing a permanent place for us, and He cannot wait until we finally make it home.

Billy Graham wrote this about heaven: "Heaven will be what we have always longed for. It will be the new social order that men dream of. All the things that have made earth unlovely and tragic will be absent in heaven. There will be no night, no death, no disease, no sorrow, no tears, no ignorance, no disappointment, no war. It will be filled with happiness, worship, love, and perfection."

If you are on vacation or a trip long enough, you begin to yearn for home. By definition, home is "the place in which one's domestic affections are centered." May my thoughts and my life represent someone whose affections are centered on Jesus and the home He is preparing for me.

Father, what does an "Eternity Mindset" mean for me today? Show me ways that I need to switch my perspective upward.

What hidden treasure did God reveal to you today? _____

_____

Do you find yourself thinking about your "forever home" in Heaven or do you think more about your "temporary home" on earth? Do you find yourself getting distracted?

_____

_____

"Since you have been raised to new life with Christ, set your sights on the realities of heaven, where Christ sits in the place of honor at God's right hand. Think about the things of heaven, not the things of earth. For you died to this life, and your life is hidden with Christ in God." Colossians 3:1-3

What is your personal interpretation of this passage from Colossians 3:1-3?

_____

_____

Your Prayer

_____

_____

A PARABLE

Let the fields and their crops burst out with joy! Let
the trees of the forest rustle with praise.
Psalm 96:12

One of the highlights of my day is taking my eight-month-old chocolate lab for a walk. We go through the wheat field and by the pond, then down through the soy bean field and end up at our favorite spot, the creek. Over the course of this week, I have noticed a beautiful flower that is coming up directly in our path. It is white, brilliant white blossom, punctuated and outlined with a bold purple. What amazed me about this flower coming up is this: it has not rained here in quite some time and the ground is extremely hard.

As I again passed by that flower this morning, God spoke to me and reminded me of how Jesus would use parables to relate, teach, and communicate with others. Little side-note, a parable is a simple story used to illustrate a moral or spiritual lesson. With this flower in mind, what was God wanting to tell me?

> **Bloom where you are planted**. The placement of this flower was one of the first things that shocked me; it was on hard, dry ground, unprotected from the August sunshine, yet thriving. Wow, how many times have I complained about a difficult 'season' that I am going through, just trying to hold it together and make it through? I definitely would not have described my attitude as "thriving!"

Be your own kind of beautiful. The beauty of the flower stood out in great contrast to its dry and dead surroundings. My spirit should be beautiful even when I am powerless over situations or circumstances surrounding me. This happens from living inside-out! No matter what is physically, emotionally, or mentally going on, our spirit can be healthy.

> "That is why we never give up. Though our bodies are dying,
> our spirits are being renewed every day." (2 Cor. 4:16)

Shine His light. That single flower had become one of the bright spots in my ordinary, daily walk; it made me think of my Creator. If I could only bring that sense of joy, wonder, and awe to someone else who is merely an observer of my life, what a wonderful witness I could be for my Father.

God spoke to me through His creation this morning: to bloom right where He places me, to find beauty in my brokenness, and to shine forth His light to brighten the paths of others. What else could He be teaching me through His creation if I would but take the time to listen?

> *Father, even creation points to You. You are amazing. Open
> my eyes so that I can see You in everything.*

What hidden treasure did God reveal to you today? _____

_____

Has God ever spoken to you through His creation?

_____

_____

God used a flower to teach me three principles:

Bloom where I am planted.
My spirit should be beautiful despite my current circumstances or surroundings.
Shine His light; let my life re-present His life.

Which one of these three principles connect the most with you, and why?

_____

_____

Your Prayer

_____

_____

JUST TELL ME WHAT TO DO

Then the Lord said to Moses, "Why are you crying out
to me? Tell the people to get moving!"
Exodus 14:15

Wait patiently for the Lord. Be brave and courageous. Yes, wait patiently for the Lord.
Psalm 27:14

"I need an answer and I really need it now! Please, God, do You hear me? Why do I feel like You are ignoring me? Are You ignoring me?"

Oh the frustration! Pray. Wait. Keep praying. Wait? Keep praying? Now what? When praying for direction in our lives, it is hard to know when to "wait on the Lord" and when to "get moving." How long are we supposed to wait before God says, "Alright, I heard you, you need to get going now." I almost wish it was like a math problem that had a formula for knowing God's will for areas of our life that cannot be found in Scripture.

Questions such as, where should I attend school? What do I need to set aside for now to focus more on my family? Should I homeschool? Am I involved in too many ministries that I cannot give a hundred percent to any of them? Does God answer our every day, sometimes simple, and sometimes complicated questions? Is He annoyed or bothered by them?

Oh, my dear one, He loves for us to come to Him with anything and everything! Nothing is too big or too small for Him. The questions are not the problem; the problem seems to be with hearing His answer. Thankfully, I am learning that sometimes, silence is also an answer. I am beginning to see that He is waiting on my move: one single step at a time, trusting that He will guide me as I lean more into Him.

When we cannot hear Him, we must not assume that He is disengaged or withholding an answer, but rather, He is asking for us to trust His silence. He is always working, always moving, and He is always on our side, working for our good and for His glory.

Father, what a personal God You are. You see me, You hear me.
What perfect peace comes in knowing that no matter what
my questions may be, You are always the Answer.

What hidden treasure did God reveal to you today? _____

_____

When was a time that you desperately needed an answer from God and it seemed that He was silent?

_____

_____

What is your thoughts on the statement: "Silence is also an answer."

_____

_____

Are there questions that you have withheld from God that you deemed "too small?"

_____

_____

Your Prayer

_____

_____

MAKE HIM GREAT

He must become greater and greater, and I must become less and less.
John 3:30

These words, spoken by John the Baptist, were in response to his disciples who were feeling the frustration of ministry. They were losing their "followers." Jesus' fame was spreading, adversely affecting John's ministry. However, John revealed his heart, the heart of his ministry, and the theme of his life in this one statement, "He must become greater and greater, and I must become less and less."

John the Baptist clearly figured out the purpose of his life. It was never to make his name known, it was never to gain the most followers, but it was to point others to Jesus.

This story, in chapter three in the book of John, exposes the brokenness of humanity: self-seeking, self-absorbed, looking out for our own best interest. What is it about the human nature that seeks and even thrives on the praises of others? We want to be noticed and appreciated. We love a pat on the back and a little bit of praise. When we do something that we perceive as good, we want some kind of recognition: If I leave a good tip, I want someone other than the waiter to know. If I read my Bible this morning and find time to pray a couple minutes, that is definitely Instagram and Facebook sharable!

However, God's kingdom does not work this way. In Matthew chapter 6, Jesus is preaching to a crowd of thousands on what is referred to as "The Sermon on the Mount." Jesus says that our good service to others (aka: our good deeds) and to His kingdom needs to be done in private. Why would He say this? Why would God ask us to make <u>His</u> Name known over having <u>our</u> name known?

No one knows our hearts, our lives, or our future better than the One who created us. He knows that true joy, lasting peace, and ultimate fulfillment only come in living for something, or should I say, Someone greater than ourselves. Let's take a moment to honestly reflect back over our lives: Did living for ourselves bring us long-term happiness?

The God of all creation has designed you to be incomplete without Him. Your innermost being cries out for God, its Creator. Going after anything else: money, material things, followers on social media, friends, will not and cannot bring any lasting peace.

As a kid in Sunday School, when the teacher would ask questions at the end of our lessons, even if we didn't pay attention, we would know that if we just answered "Jesus" to the question, nine times out of ten we would probably be right. Thirty years later, I have come to the conclusion that no matter what the problem is in life, the struggle with health, finances, friends, work, every day concerns, the answer is ALWAYS Jesus.

More of Him, less of me. God becoming greater, I becoming less; One doesn't happen without the other.

> *Father God, I do want more joy, more peace, more fulfillment in my life. I respond to the cry of my soul to return to its Creator. Become great in my life as I surrender more of myself to You.*

What hidden treasure did God reveal to you today? _____

_____

How can you apply John 3:30 to your life?

_____

_____

Do you see Jesus as the only One who can bring you long-term joy and contentment? Why or Why not? Have you been able to find it apart from Him?

_____

_____

Your Prayer

_____

_____

Day 29

NO JUDGEMENT ZONE

So don't make judgments about anyone ahead of time—before the Lord returns. For he will bring our darkest secrets to light and will reveal our private motives. Then God will give to each one whatever praise is due.
I Corinthians 4:5

I cannot stand the feeling of being judged by others! I can walk in a room and feel the pressure of judgment, based on my appearance, my friendliness (or lack of) and countless other things. So when I hear a verse that says that people are not to judge me, I instantly connect with it! I want to share this verse with all my friends, my family, neighbors, everyone!

But what about when the shoe is on the other foot? All too often as I read Scripture, I look at how well this would benefit 'so-and-so.' In Matthew 7:5 Jesus warns us of the hypocrisy of judging others:

"Hypocrite! First get rid of the log in your own eye; then you will see well enough to deal with the speck in your friend's eye."

So now let us do a little inner-directed research. It is time for personal reflection on today's Scripture. Take a second to get a deep breath because this statement from Jesus seems perfectly clear: Save the job of judgment to God.

Did you know that the Golden Rule is also in this same chapter of Matthew, just a few verses down from Jesus warning us of the danger of judging others? Verse twelve says this:

"Do to others whatever you would like them to do to you. This is the essence of all that is taught in the law and the prophets."

Talk about "summing it up!" Jesus said that the bottom line of all that the law and the prophets instructed can be as simple as doing to others as you would like them doing to you - to treat others the way you would like to be treated, and that goes for judging others as well.

Back to our verse from first Corinthians. After this brusque statement of not judging others, Paul, in his letter to the Corinthians, follows up with an even more chilling remark: "(God) will reveal our private motives." Ouch!

Here is how I interpret that: those "remarkable" things I am doing for others or for the Kingdom of God will be judged or be given praise according to the reason or purpose for *why* I was doing them. That is considered my motives.

God is in search for the pure of heart. He wants to know why am I doing these things: to be seen, to make my name known, to get a pat on the back, or to be recognized? If so, my motives are all wrong.

When I realize the mess I am on the inside, who I would be apart from Jesus in me, then I have no justifiable reason to point at anyone else in judgment. I have not been in their shoes. I recently heard Pastor Carl Lentz of Hillsong Church NYC say, "I don't need to walk in someone else's shoes, I have a mirror." That thought alone can change your entire perspective, not only in your life, but also in the lives around you.

"God sent his Son into the world not to judge the world, but to save the world through him." John 3:17

Oh Father, forgive me for making quick judgments. Forgive me of my high view of self and low view of everyone else. Let love be my highest goal.

What hidden treasure did God reveal to you today? _____

_____

I don't know of anyone who likes to be judged by others; however, we often find ourselves being the one doing the judging. Do you think this statement is true? Why or Why not?

_____

_____

_____

What practical steps can you take to stop yourself from being someone who is quick to judge?

_____

_____

_____

What are your thoughts on today's verse from first Corinthians 4:5? How do you interpret "...and (God) will reveal our private motives."

_____

_____

Your Prayer

_____

_____

FOREVER YOURS

And I am certain that God, who began the good work within you, will continue his work until it is finally finished on the day when Christ Jesus returns.
Philippians 1:6

I have a sign hanging in my hallway that says: The Best Is Yet To Come, and it is with that thought that I want to close our thirty-day journey together. Life is full of ups and downs, disappointments and triumphs, but we have the hope, as described in Philippians 1:6 that God will finish the work He has started in us and through us.

Many people say that having children gives them a view of God that they had never had before. Since my husband and I were unable to have children, God gives us other blessings to show us and teach us about Him, and one of those blessings for me is my chocolate lab, Boaz (we like to call him Bo). As I was walking with him last week, I noticed how Bo does not like me to get out of his sight. He goes sniffing one way; then a grasshopper distracts him and off he goes another way. All of a sudden, he realizes that I am out of his line-of-sight, and he instantly looks up and begins his almost frantic search for me.

As I watched Bo, God gently spoke to my heart that I am a lot like my dog. I am off and running, enjoying life, moving from one adventure to the next; however, I do get distracted and sidetracked every now and then. God revealed to me a little hidden treasure: no matter what, keep Jesus in my line-of-sight. Unlike me, Jesus can see me all the time, anywhere, everywhere; I am never hidden from Him, but I can certainly take my eyes off Him and that is where I mess up. John 15:5 says that apart from Him, I can do nothing.

With my whole heart and from my personal experience, I want to encourage you to keep your eyes, your focus, and your heart, fixed solely on Jesus. He alone is the source of true joy, perfect peace, and lasting hope. Regardless of your failures, He loves you. Despite all those who have abandoned you, He never will, and although you may not have been searching for Him, His eyes have always been on you.

He has paid a high price to love you. He exchanged the life of His Son on the chance that you would choose Him. He never has nor will He ever give up on you. The greatest treasure you will ever find is Jesus. He is the hidden treasure that your heart has been desperately searching for.

Father, my heart overflows at the lengths You have gone to, to pursue me. From this day on God, I am Yours. I give You control. I want to live my life with my eyes fixed on You, the Author and Finisher of my faith. I am forever Yours.

What hidden treasure did God reveal to you today? _____

_____

Do you feel consistent in keeping Jesus in your "line-of-sight?" Explain your answer.

_____

_____

_____

What do you think John 15:5 means when Jesus says that "apart from Him I can do nothing?"

_____

_____

Knowing Jesus chose you and that He will never leave you or abandon you is a treasure worth more than gold. Write a prayer of thanksgiving to your Father who has sought you out, paid a high price to call you His, and loves you more than you could ever fathom.

Your Prayer

_____

_____

WARNING: Reading any further could alter the future of your life!

I want to personally extend an invitation to you; an invitation to come alongside me and countless others as we intentionally live out our faith. Join us as we live a life in pursuit of God; but God also has an invitation for you as well.

God's Invitation: accept His request to come into your life. God wants to help you live your life to the fullest. God wants to heal your brokenness, He deeply desires a relationship with you; but He will only come into your life, into your heart, if you ask Him. He is waiting even now with open arms.

First, you have to realize your need for help. You need of a Savior. "For everyone has sinned; we all fall short of God's glorious standard" (Romans 3:23). "No one is righteous – not even one" (Romans 3:10).

The second thing you have to do - believe. Simple as that. "If you openly declare that Jesus is Lord and believe in your heart that God raised him from the dead, you will be saved. For it is believing in your heart that you are made right with God, and it is openly declaring your faith that you are saved" (Romans 10:9-10).

"For everyone who calls on the name of the Lord will be saved." (Romans 10:13)

If you just accepted His invitation, let me be the first to welcome you to the Family! You belong here - no more SEARCHING.

A Note from the Author

Thank you for taking this thirty-day journey with me. I want to encourage you to keep pressing in, to keep staying in pursuit of the Father's heart. There is nothing in this world that will satisfy you like He will and there is nothing in the world that will fulfill you and complete you like His love will. He is the greatest treasure of all.

When I was a little girl, I loved to crawl up on my dad's lap, letting his arms surround me; I felt safe, protected, and completely loved. This is His invitation to you: He invites you to crawl up into His lap and breathe in deeply as He holds you, comforts you, and affirms His love to you. Live your life from this position - knowing that you are completely and forever loved.

This is your home…in His arms.

You are safe here. You are whole here. You are in an intimate relationship with God, and this is the reason you were created. When you rest in this place, you no longer feel lacking, no longer feel incomplete, no longer feel unloved, or insignificant.

With Him, you are whole. With Him, you are the truest version of yourself. In His arms, you begin to see yourself as He sees you: beautiful and loved.

Let this be the day that you can look back on and know "This is where my life changed. This is the day I was no longer satisfied with being average. I am 'All In!' I am living my life in pursuit of knowing Him more."

Printed in the United States
By Bookmasters